Signs, Wonders and Miracles will follow those who Believe

John Beech

Copyright © 2022 by John Beech

All rights reserved. No part of this publication may be reproduced, stored in a retrieval system, or transmitted in any form or by any means without prior written permission from the author, except for brief quotations used in printed reviews.

Unless otherwise indicated, scripture quotations are taken from the New King James Bible, copyright 1982 by Thomas Nelson, Inc. Used by Permission.

Credits: Cover design, editing, and interior design by Kathy Mayo

ISBN-Soft Cover: 9798360664352

First edition: October, 2022

Publisher: John Beech
Contact John: beechnut383@gmail.com

Printed in the United States of America

Contents

Dedication 5
About Author 6
Foreword 8
Related Bible Scriptures 9

PART 1
  Personal Testimonials 11
    God's Road Trips 12
    What Fibromyalgia? 15
    Healing Through Repentance 17
    Miracle Baby 20
    Mystery Door Miracles 23
    Smoke No More 27
    Money Manifested 29
    The Squirrel 30
    Sneaky Snake 32
    Handicapped for Life 34
    Not Just One...Multiple Healings 38
    A Hoarder's Hands 42
    All Needs Met! 44
    Injury, Cancer, Pain - Miraculous Healings . . . 45
    Skin Cancer Healed 51
    Eyesight Restored 52
    Even Trees Obey 53

Praying in the Spirit 57
Conference Miracles 57
Hernia Healed 64
College Mission 65
Knee Repaired in a Store 67
Healing Lunch 71
Medication Miracle 73
Bye-Bye Demons! 74
Tongue-Tie Healing 79
Dead Battery Challenge 81
Faulty Brakes 83
Rapid Weight Loss 85
Dad's Stroke - Seizures 87
*Be Careful Who Your Friends Are
   Because You May Become Like Them* . . 89
Miraculous Healings 95
Knee Problem 98
More Than Enough God 99
David Hogan 101
*About John Beech – Life Story
   (as of September 17, 2022)* 102

In closing... 115

PART 2
 Plan of Salvation 116

PART 3
 Receive the Holy Spirit 118

Dedication

I dedicate this book to the Lord Jesus Christ for showing me how to pray for the sick, how to trust Him in all things, and to believe that I can do what He did—and more—because He said so.

When the Holy Spirit taught me how to pray in the Spirit (praying in tongues), I began a whole new personal relationship with Him. He gave me boldness while talking to people, and I am quicker to repent when I do wrong. The Holy Spirit taught me to love people and to have compassion for the lost and hurting.

The Holy Spirit taught me to stop thinking small, but rather think big! He gave me a vision so big that I could never achieve it without Him. The Holy Spirit told me to believe Him to fund and accomplish my big vision.

About Author

My life changed when I surrendered my life to Jesus Christ on May 3, 1979. And then later when I learned about being baptized in the Holy Spirit and praying in tongues, WOW, what a change that brought to my life!

It has been 12 years since the Holy Spirit began teaching me so much. He gave me the boldness to talk to anyone about Jesus. When I pray in the Spirit and then listen for His voice, the Holy Spirit talks to me. I ask Him how to pray for the sick, He tells me, I pray, and then He heals them.

The Holy Spirit has been showing me many new things. He has even told me to stop eating certain foods, what foods to eat, and what supplements to take for optimum health. My relationship with the Holy Spirit is very important to me!

Because of my surrendered life and personal relationship with Jesus, I learned to repent quickly when I sin.

When I read the Bible, God reveals things to me that I had never known or seen before. When the Holy Spirit tells me to do something, I have learned to quickly obey, and the results are amazing!

I often sing to Jesus, and He even told me that He has some favorite songs that He likes me to sing to Him.

I asked the Holy Spirit to allow me, during my lifetime, to witness people's sick or broken body parts healed or recreated, people raised from the dead, people delivered from infirmities, demons cast out, and miraculous unusual miracles. I also greatly desire to see millions come to know and surrender their lives to Jesus Christ by my influencing-ministering to them.

Thank you, Father, for hearing and answering my prayers.

~ John Beech

Foreword

Ever since I met John, he has been a personal guide in prayer-warrior-living, in praying in the Spirit, and crushing every assignment of the enemy. He has a powerful heart for all to walk in daily relationship with God and hearing His voice. John's heart for God is bold and infectious. He zealously points all he encounters to a supernatural and holy God as he seeks everyone to join in our heavenly future.

John seeks to share what he has learned about a moment-by-moment, one day at a time, garden-walk with our Creator and realize the freedom that flows from it. As you read this book, I'm sure you will realize the pure excitement John has for what God is doing and is going to do for all who seek him. Read it, devour it, and let it show you more of God's heart!

~ Paul Martin, Life of Pursuit Ministries

I have been honored and extremely blessed by God choosing me to help John bring his book to life! God has touched my heart through every one of John's testimonials, and this book is truly a faith-building tool that has changed my Spiritual beliefs in the power of prayer and has strengthened my personal relationship with God!

~ Kathy Mayo, Editor

Related Bible Scriptures

¹²"Most assuredly, I say to you, he who believes in me the works that I do he will do also and greater works than these will he do because I go to my father. ¹³And whatever you ask in my name, that I will do, that the father may be glorified in the son. ¹⁴If you ask anything in my name, I will do it. ¹⁵If you love me, keep my commandments."

— John 14:12-15

"But the helper, the Holy Spirit, whom the Father will send in my name. He will teach you all things and bring to your remembrance all things that I said to you."

— John 14:26

"If you abide in me and my words abide in you, you will ask what you desire, and it shall be done for you."

— John 15:7

"You did not choose me, but I chose you and appointed you that you should go bear fruit, and your fruit should remain, that whatever you ask the father in my name he may give you."

— John 15:16

Signs, Wonders, and Miracles

Hear and Obey His Voice

Part 1

Personal Testimonials

I'm sharing these true testimonial stories with you for several reasons—the first and most important is because God told me to share them.

I believe that through these stories, God will reveal the importance of a surrendered life and a personal relationship with Him.

I pray that He also uses these stories to further reveal the power, blessings, healings, and happiness that come from surrendering your life to Him.

I pray that you will open your hearts and minds as you read these examples of how God has been using me to touch and change lives, and how He wants to use you in the same ways.

Allow these stories to touch your life and encourage you to make the most important decision of your life—to make God the Lord of your life.

God's Road Trips

One day God asked me to go to a city located two states away from home. I didn't have any money to go...literally none with me or in any of my accounts, but my fuel tank was full, and I was ready to obey God's calling.

I invited a friend to come along because I don't feel comfortable going into some areas alone. I also wanted this to be a teaching opportunity to show him how the Kingdom of God operates.

I knew we had enough fuel to get there and to do what God wanted us to do, but I wasn't confident that we would have enough fuel to return home. I told my friend that I didn't have any money, but that when God tells you to go someplace, you go, and then He's the one who makes sure you get there and back.

We drove around in certain neighborhoods and college campuses where God led us in this particular city. We prayed and sometimes He had me sing—He does have favorite songs, after all, He's the one who creates these things. We accomplished all that God had sent us to do over an 8-hour period of driving.

Up until that time, my friend hadn't seen too many miracles but his faith was growing through this God-assigned road trip. I didn't have a map or GPS; we just followed God's direction, literally, which was like GPS directions...turn here, turn there, drive so far, etc..

It was getting late, and I was exhausted from driving and praying for hours. My friend told me to keep praying and he would drive!

As we drove through certain areas, the demonic presence was so heavy that we could tangibly feel it. We literally saw evil leave those places. And then when we left those areas, we felt the heaviness lift.

One time God told me that wherever He directs me to go, He is busting up the atmosphere because His glory is getting ready to come! And I totally believe that His glory is going to shine out onto every single person on the planet. And then they will have the chance to accept Jesus or not to. I hope that, if you're not already saved, that you would come to Jesus.

As we were driving down the freeway, my friend said, "Wow, look at the traffic jam up ahead!" The cars were backed up for miles, as far as we could see! I looked at the fuel gauge and it was pretty low. So he said he would drive in the outside lane in case we did run out of gas we could easily push the car over onto the shoulder. Well, I told him, "We're not going to run out of gas, because if God brought us down here to pray, then He is going to get us home. I don't care if there is gas in the tank or not, somehow it is going to work."

We were driving along and I was starting to nod off...just being honest, I was tired! All of a sudden he starts to hoot and holler and carry on. I asked, "What's the matter?" He said, "Look at the gas gauge!" We watched God increase our gas and raised our gas gauge to a quarter of a tank, and then it stopped.

My friend asked why God hadn't filled the tank all the way. I said that God isn't done teaching us something. Over the remainder of our trip back home, we watched God add gas in our tank three times that night...quarter of a tank at a time. That is God taking care of His kids!

If God tells you to go and do something, or if He tells you to go give all your money away, or whatever it is...do it! Drive to that place, do what He says to do, and He will totally bless you. It might not come back right away, but sometimes it does.

I give all the praise, glory and honor to Jesus for what He did for us!

Thank you Jesus!

What Fibromyalgia?

God revealed to me that Fibromyalgia affects some men, but mostly women after they experience trauma, such as getting a divorce or having been involved in an automobile accident.

God taught me that when we pray for someone with Fibromyalgia, and we command that trauma to leave in Jesus' name, the effects of the *trauma* leaves the body, and so does the Fibromyalgia.

One day Jesus led me into a business showroom where a salesman approached me and asked if he could help me. I was looking for a Hi-Lo at that time, so he showed me their Hi-Lo, and then we struck up a "personal" conversation.

I told him I was a Christian and that I pray for people, and then Jesus heals them. I asked if there was anything I could pray with him about. He told me that he had recently been told that he had Fibromyalgia and was experiencing all the typical pain that is associated with the disease.

Before his sales job, this man was an electrician but he had to give up that career because of the pain. I told him that Jesus was the healer, and then explained to him that Fibromyalgia attacks mostly women, and that he was the first man I had met who suffers from it.

He told me that he went through a bitter divorce and that this disease and pain came on him about six months after. I asked him if I could pray for him, and he said yes, so I commanded Fibromyalgia and pain and trauma to leave his body in the name of Jesus.

I then asked him how he was feeling. He started moving around as joy came to his face. He started jumping around yelling, "The pain is gone!" Many other employees jumped up in their work areas to see what was going on. He kept yelling, "I'm healed! Thank you, Jesus, I'm healed." He said he was going to return to doing electrical work because he enjoyed it more than his sales job.

That man was a believer in Jesus Christ. That day, Jesus showed me that if I am willing and obedient, He will use me everywhere I go.

Praise the Lord!

Personal Testimonials

Healing Through Repentance

One of my friends took one of her friends to the hospital because she had extreme pain in her right flank. They kept her there for several hours, did a lot of scans and blood work, but couldn't find anything wrong with her. So my friend called her husband, and he told her to call me to ask me to pray for her. We were both driving at the time, so I pulled over and waited for my friend and her friend to arrive where I was.

I didn't know the woman for whom I would be praying, so I asked God how to pray for her. *He is the healer, I am not.* So I literally prayed as God told me to do, and the pain subsided a bit, but it didn't go away altogether; that wasn't normal. So I again went before God and asked Him, "What is going on here?" God gave me a word of knowledge that the girl has unforgiveness. So I told her that she has to repent and renounce whatever unforgiveness she is hanging onto, and that she didn't have to say it out loud or to me, but that it was just between her and God.

She did as I told her, and then I prayed for her again. Like last time, the pain subsided a little more, but it wasn't totally gone. So, I went back to God and asked, "What's going on?" I heard from Him again, and I conveyed what He had told me, "God told me that you feel guilty for the way you raised your children and that you are hanging on to that guilt which is causing you to have all this pain. God says that you need to repent for what you did that's causing all the guilt."

She told me that her children don't really know Jesus Christ as their Savior because she had led them into a religion that was "just a religion." I said, "That's all you knew at the time, but now you've given your heart to Jesus. You need to pray for the children, but it's not your responsibility to get them saved. You can't save a fly, just like I can't heal a fly with a broken wing; it's all done by Jesus Christ." So she repented for taking on the blame for raising her kids the way she did.

I'm not kidding...as she was renouncing and asking God to forgive her for that, I could feel the Holy Spirit on me and I started to weep under the presence of God, and so was she. As soon as she was done, and I said, "Be healed in Jesus' name," the pain was instantly gone!

A lot of times there are things in your life that have become blocks to your healings. But once you ask God to forgive you for those things—most of the time you know what they are—the healing comes a whole lot quicker.

I just want to emphasize that if you are carrying any guilt, anger, bitterness, unforgiveness, or anything like that, and you are suffering with a sickness, ask God to forgive you, and He will. Or ask God to come into your life as your Lord and

Personal Testimonials

Savior if you don't even know Him. Or ask Him to reveal Himself to you, and I'm telling you, He will. *And then you can give your heart to Jesus.*

Miracle Baby

I think God has a great sense of humor. He has asked me to go to many unknown places, do many unusual tasks, and led me into situations that seemed very strange. But always with purpose, of which I discover when I obey!

Some time ago, God asked me to go to a particular store and sit in an area where I could enjoy coffee and food before shopping. He told me He was going to send people to *me* who needed healing.

God said that if I would ask the Holy Spirit how to pray for them, *and I obeyed*, He would heal them. He told me I needed to stay one hour a day; I said OK, and I did as He directed me.

On the first day, a lady sat within three feet of me and then started telling me what was wrong with her; she had Fibromyalgia. After I prayed, Jesus healed her of that disease and she went away laughing. The Holy Spirit was all over that woman and I could hear her laughing all across the store.

Then an Asian woman with her 8-month-old baby son approached and asked if they could share the table with me. Her boy was so cute, and she told me that she wanted another baby but her son was adopted and they could not afford another $38,000 expense that would be required to adopt another child until she and her husband finished paying the adoption expenses for this baby boy.

I told her I was a Christian, and that Jesus heals people when I pray for them. I asked if I could pray for her, and she said yes. I asked her if I could hold her hand, and she agreed, and then I asked the Holy Spirit to tell me how to pray.

I heard the Holy Spirit say that she had painful fibroids in her womb which were preventing her from getting pregnant. So I told her what the Holy Spirit had told me, and she was very surprised. She asked, "How do you know that?" I told her the Holy Spirit told me, and then she said He is right because she had just been given the same diagnosis that week. So I prayed for her and commanded the fibroids to dissolve in Jesus' name.

I then asked if she was feeling something because of the shocked look on her face. She said she felt heat and it felt like someone had both hands in her belly moving things around. Then she said, "WOW, I feel the fibroids dissolving like clumps of Epsom salts in water. I have never felt so good." Her face was just glowing.

I told this woman that the Holy Spirit gave me a personal word for her. He said that it was springtime and that she should go home and plant lots of seeds because she is going to have a baby. As she left, she thanked me for praying and thanked Jesus for healing her.

I encountered her again 13 months later in that same store. She excitedly, and loudly, exclaimed, "Thank you, and thank You Jesus! Look at my new baby girl!" WOW, she was so beautiful—this miracle made me cry as well.

God had me pray for 47 women in that store, all had different forms of these fibroids in their wombs, and some had hormone issues as well. Jesus healed them all.

I thank You, King Jesus.

Mystery Door Miracles

When I learned how to pray in the Spirit, a real boldness came on me to the point where I was OK if I looked like a fool before God and man. I simply obey Him.

As I said in the past, the Lord leads me to different places to pray for people, and one day God led me to a business about 3:00 p.m. during their shift change. I followed the Lord's leading to a side door, and then sat in my car praying in the Spirit, asking the Lord what I was supposed to do there. I don't always know why He directs me to specific places, so I was being patient and waited for Him to direct me again.

I saw a lady drive up and she parked her car next to me. It was a black car, and I saw the lady go into the side door, and then I heard God say, "That's who I want you to pray for."

I walked in the door, and to my surprise there were three locked doors in front of me. I couldn't go where the woman went, I couldn't get into the warehouse, and I couldn't get back out. So I rang a door bell in front of me, and a security guard approached me. I said, "I don't know the woman's name, she owns that black car out there, and she just walked into this building. I was sent by the Lord Jesus Christ to pray for her. Is there any way I could talk to her?" He said yes and told me her name. He went in there, spoke to her, and brought her out to me. I explained to her that I was a Christian and that the Lord leads me to pray for people who He wants to touch.

This woman was Catholic, and she started telling me her story, and it was just heartbreaking. She had lost her grandfather, her son, and her husband all in the same month, from different causes. And then she developed fibromyalgia and heart problems, along with four other health issues, all within the last six months. Also she had been diagnosed with terminal breast cancer just a week earlier.

I said God sent me here to pray for you, and He is going to heal you of all of it. So God had me pray against all the trauma, and that joy and peace would come back into her life, and some other issues that we dealt with. The Lord's presence was so strong that both of us were weeping, and she was just praising the Lord. She was a Christian lady and knew without a shadow of a doubt that this was a God-appointment for her.

I kid you not...as I was talking with her, she could feel the cancerous tumors leave her body. Peace came over her; her face glowed like there was a light behind it, and she was happy and at peace. She no longer carried the guilt of being a survivor.

The security guard came back in and saw that she was emotional and crying. He asked if everything was all right with her, and she said, "Absolutely! God is here and God is healing me." He looked at her with a surprised look, turned around and walked away.

For about 30 minutes after I finished talking, God continued to minister to her. And I'm telling you...it was like He peeled years off that woman, and the stresses just left her. She was at absolute total peace. She felt good in her body. She was in some pain before, but everything went away. Arthritis went away along with a whole list of problems—they all literally went away.

She said, "I can feel the cancerous tumors leave and the pain and discomfort leave, and I just feel absolutely incredible." She was trembling. When the presence of God gets on a person, sometimes they laugh uncontrollably, sometimes they cry, sometimes nothing happens, and sometimes they tremble. It was absolutely incredible what God did for that woman.

And then, when the healings were completed, she said, "Thank you for being so brave to walk into a place like this and pray for me." I responded, "God tells me to do things and I am quick to obey. I am not perfect, but I am quick to obey. "

She gave me half a dozen hugs, we shook hands, and then we parted ways. But I'm telling you...God changed that woman! It was incredible what God did.

After I left and got into my car, I was going to start the car when God said, "Just a minute," then He gave me a word. He said, "I want to thank you, John, for obeying me, and doing what I tell you to do." That just made me cry!

We don't know all the affects of what He does to people. *I just praise God for all that He does, in Jesus' name.*

Personal Testimonials

Smoke No More

One hot summer day, I walked into a coffee shop/thrift store. I noticed a guy who was standing about six feet from me because I heard him breathing; his lungs sounded very junky.

I asked him if he was a smoker, and he said yes. I asked how many packs a day he smoked. He said four packs a day. I said WOW, that's a lot. I mentioned that it is an expensive habit, and he agreed. He said he had tried everything to quit but he hadn't been able to.

I told him that I was a Christian and that I pray for people, and then Jesus heals them. I asked him if he would like me to pray for him. He said yes, and he told me that he was a new Christian. I put my hand on his shoulder and asked the Holy Spirit how He wanted me to pray. Then I stood still, listening for His direction.

Sometimes healings require action by the person being prayed for, and this was one of those cases. I told him that this is what God told me to tell him: "You are going to smoke again, don't worry about that. Every time you take a drag on a cigarette, just say 'Thank You, Jesus, that I don't smoke anymore. Continue to repeat the phrase 'thank You, Jesus, that I don't smoke anymore' *until you stop smoking.* God said as you do this by faith, He is going to make it taste so bad that you *will* stop smoking." Then I prayed for all damage to his lungs to be healed in Jesus' name.

He began weeping because Jesus touched this man and he said, "I can breathe freely. All the junkie lung stuff left because of Jesus Christ."

That man did what Jesus told him to do, and he stopped his 4-packs-a-day habit in just three weeks.

He admitted that it was hard to do at first, but then he decided he really did want Jesus to heal him. He thanked me for obeying God and for going where God tells me to go.

Thanks again, King Jesus, for using me. I love You so much.

Money Manifested

I was walking on the street and the Lord told me to stop and give all the money I had with me to a homeless woman, and then I was to give her a word of knowledge from God. He told me to tell her, "He loves her very much, and that within the year she will not be on the street anymore."

I only had a ten and two twenty dollar bills in my wallet. I was on my way to join some friends for dinner, so I didn't have extra money to give to her, but still God told me to give it to her. So I obeyed; I gave her the money, and then gave her the specific word from the Lord.

It really touched the woman and she started to weep. I was happy to give it to her, but on the same token, now I didn't have any money to go out to dinner with my friends. So I got in the car and was going to call my friends to reschedule when God told me to look in my wallet. I looked and there it was...the same ten and two twenty dollar bills showed up back in my wallet.

So God showed me a manifestation of money in my wallet, which was pretty amazing!

And I just give God all the Praise and honor and glory for it, in Jesus' name!

The Squirrel

The Holy Spirit often prompts me to drive around into unknown areas, and then He directs me to people to whom He wants me to minister.

On one such occasion, the Holy Spirit had me driving to an unfamiliar area, and while I was praying in the Spirit, a squirrel ran out in front of my car. I couldn't avoid hitting and killing the poor small animal.

I felt really bad so I went back, put my finger on its head, and prayed for life to come back into its body. I also prayed that it wouldn't remember the trauma of being hit.

I didn't see it move at all, but that didn't matter to me because I was practicing praying and believing!

I continued to drive for about a mile, all the while praying, and then God had me turn around again. I continued praying and driving as I returned to the accident site. I looked for the squirrel, but it was not there. I got out and looked in the ditches and all around the area, but there was no squirrel to be found.

I believe God raised that squirrel from the dead, just like He says we can do when we pray, *trusting Him* for the fulfilling answer. It was truly a faith-building experience.

*"Most assuredly, I say to you, he who believes
in me the works that I do he will do also
and greater works than these will he
do because I go to my father."*

— *John 14:12*

Sneaky Snake

I was at church the other day with three of my friends, and one of them was having extreme neck and arm pain on her left side. It had been bothering her for a week and the pain was just horrific. She told me what was wrong and wanted to be delivered from it.

I shared with her about how God deals with me. I was in sales, selling flooring, and I would go into a person's home, and literally within 5-15 minutes of me being in the house, someone in the home would tell me about something that was wrong with them or with their kids. That was a 'red flag' to me to pray for those people after I was through showing them the products which they had asked me there to see.

About a week before the encounter with this lady at the church, God had taught me how to pray differently for people. It's been incredible! I saw God deliver three people instantly because of this method of praying.

So once again I went to God and asked Him how I should pray for this lady. He told me that she has unforgiveness toward one particular person. I asked her if it was true, and she agreed it was. I told her that she needed to renounce that unforgiveness and repent, and forgive that person. So she did, and then I prayed for her. The

Personal Testimonials

woman began slithering on the ground just like a snake...it was incredible. So I bound up that demon spirit and I commanded that demon in her to be driven out by the name of Jesus Christ and His blood.

That demon manifested for a couple minutes, and then I told it to get out again. And it did! And then God spoke to me again and told me that she's a control freak (bluntly) and that she wants to be in control too much. I told her that she has got to give that to Jesus, because it hurts her and her family, and it is not from God, and that it is actually a slavery mentality. So she did repent, and she forgave herself as well. I prayed for her again, and it was totally gone...that demon left her!

Afterward, her face looked as though she was 10 years younger. She was full of joy, she had peace, and she was happy! And she felt even better when I contacted her within the following week.

God did an incredible thing in that woman's life. I give God all the praise, honor, and glory for it!

Handicapped for Life

I took care of my mother and father until they passed away, and I was burned out from all of it. I just lay on the floor and cried out to God asking, "What should I do now?" I heard Him say to trust Him. Sometime later, the Lord gave me a witty idea for an invention so I started a business, and then I literally chased God for three years in doing what I needed to do in my day-to-day life and for the invention.

I totally relied on Him for a place to lay my head and for money. It was incredible what He did in those three years. During that time, God directed me multiple times to a store where He wanted me to pray for people. That is where God told me that I would be writing a book, and He gave me the inspiration for it. I believed Him, and this book was birthed.

It's kind of hard to explain how God leads me, but one day He basically told me to turn into a driveway of two small strips malls with an empty space between them. In the second strip mall there was a church, coffee house, and resale type shop all in the same place. As soon as I drove in I saw a guy in a window who jumped up like he was really excited!

I told God, "Well, this ought to be interesting." I went up to the door and the guy shook my hand...

he was the assistant pastor at that small church. We chit-chatted a little bit and then, literally, this pastor told me that for 3-1/2 years he had prayed for a guy like me to walk through the door because he wanted to learn how to pray for people. He knew how to pray in the Spirit, but he didn't know how to pray for people to see them healed.

There were a couple other people there with the pastor. One was a young man who was afflicted with medical issues from an aneurism since he was six years old. It had really messed him up. One of his legs was literally 10 inches shorter than the other, and his left arm from the elbow down to his hand was twisted around, maybe twice, and then upside-down from what it should be. It's difficult to explain how mangled it was.

The pastor was right there, got me a cup of coffee, and I said to him, "I'm going to teach you what you need to do. I asked that boy if he knew Jesus Christ as his Lord and Savior. He said yes, and then told me about when he was saved and became a Christian. When we become Christians, God gives us all the authority to do the same signs, wonders and miracles that He did.

I held up one of the boy's legs and another person held up the other leg, and I told the pastor to command that leg to grow out in Jesus' name!

He did...and he was absolutely floored! I thought we would have to pick him up off the floor because he was so dumbfounded that the leg obeyed! Like I said, it was 10 inches shorter than the other, and we all saw it grow out even with the other leg.

I asked the pastor and the boy, "Do you want to see something funny?" They both agreed! I told them that God has a sense of humor, and I then commanded that leg to grow out another four inches...and it did! So now it's four inches longer than the 'normal' leg and I move away as though I was just going to walk away. The boy said, "No, no, I can't walk like this." I chuckled, and then commanded the leg to go back the four inches where it should be, and it did.

That boy was squirming in his chair while the leg was growing out, and he was shocked because God was re-aligning his whole pelvis with his spine, straightening everything that was crooked in that area. That boy was just squirming in his chair and was shocked at the same time.

This boy had never worked a day in his life because of his disabilities, so I had the pastor pray for the boy's arm too. We literally watched God totally unwind that arm! I've never seen anything like it myself. I've seen many legs grow out many times, but I've never seen an unraveling of an arm. It was so incredible to witness.

The arm straightened to a certain position, not quite normal, and then it just stopped straightening. The pastor asked, "Why did it stop?" I replied, "I don't know why it stopped." In order to find out why it stopped, we prayed again, but it didn't straighten any further. But the boy, incredibly, walked totally normal.

So I sought the Lord, fasted, and prayed for a few days after that, and then God gave me the reason the arm didn't totally straighten. I called the pastor and conveyed God's answer to him. Since the boy had never worked a day in his life, he wouldn't know where to begin to find a job. And because all his housing, his food, insurances, literally everything was paid for by his Disability benefits, he didn't want to be totally healed for fear of losing all that.

Well, within probably six months after that I saw that boy. Because of his fears of not knowing how to get a job and losing his Disability benefits, all the healing that had taken place the day we prayed for him had all been reversed to the ways they were because he would rather be handicapped than be healed.

That was so sad to witness. But I cannot override someone who does not want healing, or someone who wants to die either. God says in His word that if a person wants to die that's their choice.

All I know is that I obeyed God's leading and that pastor learned about praying for healings that day. No one can take that experience and teaching from us.

Praise You Jesus!

Not Just One...Multiple Healings

In the same church and day that we prayed for the handicapped boy *(in the previous story 'Handicapped for Life')*, there was an elderly woman using a walker while shopping, and her hands and legs were all crippled. She stopped to have a cup of coffee, and the pastor introduced me to her as one of the church members.

I was talking to her, having a good conversion, and I asked her, "What's the scoop with you, why are you all crippled up?" She told me that she had a destructive rheumatoid arthritis type thing going on. She was in a lot of pain, and her fingers were crooked, and just totally not right.

I said, "It's a lot of pain, huh?" She said, "Oh yes, its extreme pain. I take pills for it all the time."

So we continued chit-chatting, having our coffee, and I said, "You know, Jesus is the healer." In instances like this, I generally will share a testimony or two about others I've seen healed in their condition; it helps to build up their faith. I was doing that with this lady, and I asked her, "How would you like to walk again without the walker, and have your fingers and legs and everything straighten out like they are supposed to be?" She said, "Well, that would be wonderful!"

Personal Testimonials

I prayed for that lady, and the pastor watched as all the pain went away immediately. I then said, "Let's go for a walk." She stood up...real slow. I said, "That's not right, sit back down." In the Bible it states that Jesus prayed for a blind man three separate times, which gives us hope that we can pray for someone more than once to see a miracle. So I prayed for that lady again.

I prayed that her legs would straighten out, and that the energy and vitality of her youth would come back to her. And I am telling you... when I asked her to get up and walk a second time, she leaped up off that chair and stood! It was amazing!

Then I told her, "I'd like you to walk a little bit with the walker, and then I want you to walk with me." So she walked with the walker for about five feet, and then she grabbed onto my arm and we started to walk together. The more we walked the straighter her legs got. Also her fingers were moving, cracking, popping, and straightening. It was awesome to watch God heal this woman progressively right in front of us. And pretty soon, she let go of my arm and started running around the sanctuary of the church. And I mean, really running! She made three laps around there and came back and said, "I feel absolutely incredible!"

I told her she needed to thank Jesus. So she stood there, praising the Lord with her arms lifted up, thanking God for healing her. She sat back down and I sat and talked with her.

The pastor was there along with some others who had come by, and they were all in awe of what God was doing in that place. It was miraculous!

I told the lady, "God just told me something... you don't have a whole lot of time left in life since you are up in the years, so don't you think that since God healed your body that it's time that you gave your heart to Him." The pastor said, "Oh, no, no, no, she's saved. She's been coming here for five years." I responded, "That's not what God told me." Then I asked her, "You're not saved, are you?" "No, I'm not," she replied.

The pastor said, "What!? But you do this, this, and this..."

She said, "Yes, I do. It's called 'playing church'. I'm not saved, but I want to be."

And I had the privilege of leading this woman to the Lord right there in that pastor's church. I believe that in every single church, there are people sitting in the pews that we know, or are our friends, and we think they are saved but they are not.

I believe that with all of my heart. I've seen it more than once. I used to be that kind of a guy. I was raised in a church, and I sat in that chair for many years pretending to be a Christian, and I wasn't saved. Deep down, I knew it, but everybody around me thought I was saved because I knew all the Christian words...the sayings the way you do around Christians and all that 'junk'. All that was just religion, and religion will get you to hell really quick.

So I would give you a word that you need to give your heart to Jesus, just like that woman did. She gave her heart to Jesus and the joy of the Lord came on her, and she hooted and hollered and danced all around. It was amazing.

For the next 4-1/2 hours, every single person that came through that door who were sick or had anything wrong with them, God healed them! And I mean immediately!

That pastor was just beside himself at how easy it was because he had always thought it was hard, and he had gotten himself into a box. Headaches were healed, aches and pains were healed, eyesight was healed, a numerous amount of afflictions were healed, and trauma that a person had experienced from abuse. God healed it all within 4-1/2 hours.

God had me attend that church for a month, and then He told me to leave. He had other plans for me from then on.

So don't put God in a box, step out in faith, and just go for it!

A Hoarder's Hands

One summer, I was invited to a friend's house for lunch along with a group of other guys who were invited. One was a missionary pastor and the rest were friends and business acquaintances of the host.

While I was outside, another guy pulled up and we started a conversation. I asked him, "What's caused your hands to be afflicted with your fingers all crooked and stiff. He told me that, at one time, he had been into witchcraft. Then God began revealing to me what was going on with him.

I asked him, "Would you like me to pray for you?" He said, "Yes," so I asked the Lord how to pray for the man. God showed me that the man was a hoarder, so I asked the guy point blank if he was a hoarder; he said, "Yes." So we talked about that for a little bit, and then I told him that he needed to ask God to forgive him for being a hoarder because that is not of God. Having pathways through your house is not from God, and that the enemy comes to kill, steal, and destroy.

I prayed over this man, and I watched as God totally, radically, changed his hands. His fingers straightened out, and he could now clench his hands into fists. Prior to this healing, he could hardly hang onto his steering wheel, and basically had to navigate the steering wheel with his thumbs because his other fingers were so stiff he couldn't move them at all.

I told him, "Now you need to give Jesus all the praise, honor and glory for all that God just did for you." So we went into the house and got to eating dinner, and talking and whatnot. The others were just amazed at how God had just healed this man's hands. God was the talk of the table, giving Him honor and glory.

Afterward, one of the business guys said, "I have never heard of anything like that before," and then handed me a $100 bill to continue doing ministry.

What God had done there was pretty amazing!

All Needs Met!

As I was out and about one day, I was standing outside of my car when a guy approached me. We began chit-chatting and he said, "The Lord told me that you need money for your car insurance." I said, "Yes, I do."

We chit-chatted for a few more minutes, and then that guy handed me $1,000 to pay for six months of insurance coverage.

That was such a blessing to me, and is just one of many examples of how He proves He takes care of ALL my (our) needs, according to His riches and glory in Christ Jesus.

His promises are always Yes and Amen!

Personal Testimonials

Injury, Cancer, Pain Miraculous Healings

In year 2000, I was working at a Rescue Mission and I was on the side of a building on a scaffold 12 feet off the ground putting up an awning so people were protected from rain and snow.

The scaffolding gave way and I rode it down, but got pinned between the railing and scaffold and the decking. I was stuck and couldn't get out. My buddy was on up on another ladder, and we had run a long board across between the two ladders to be able to hook the awning onto the brick wall. There were five other guys working on the building at the time, and they all ran over to help me; they all helped me get out of that thing.

I was hurt pretty badly, so I went into the bathroom to see what kind of damage I had done to myself. I was skinned from my chest all the way to my ankles. My buddy drove me to the hospital where I found out that I blew out a couple discs in my back and caused damage to my kidney that resulted in surgery to repair. It's the only time a doctor told me it was a good thing that I was a fat guy because the damage could have been much worse.

I was in extremely horrific pain for about three months; the type of pain where you feel like you would almost be better off dead because it was so bad! I had to get shots in my back in the Transcutaneous Electrical Nerve Stimulation (TENS) unit. I prayed and I prayed for myself. At that time I didn't know anything about praying for healing yet. I didn't yet know about praying in tongues either.

What I didn't realize at that time was, because of the 'junk' that I was into, not really living for the Lord yet, that I had brought the spirit of death into my life. I used to enjoy a song with my friends, "Highway to Hell," and believe me…if I had stayed with those friends I probably would have been in hell because we narrowly escaped several head-on crashes that could have happened very easily.

You need to check out very carefully who your friends are, because not everyone who claims to be your friends are your friends. If they're not leading you closer to Jesus, but leading you closer to the pit, you need to get rid of them.

I suffered with that back pain for years, but I just didn't know about healing.

Then in 2001, I was working at the same Rescue Mission when I wasn't feeling well, so I went to the doctor. He ran some tests and found out that I had Blast Cell Leukemia and advanced Prostate Cancer that had gone into my bones and liver. The doctor ordered a series of scans, and the tests revealed that I had a tumor the size of an egg on my liver.

Personal Testimonials

Of course, the first thing the doctors wanted to do was cut my prostate out and cut my liver open to get that tumor out. But the tumor was in the bone and I was experiencing absolute horrendous pain from that. I prayed about the decision, and my closest friends all prayed about it for me as well. I felt led to go to a medical practice in Georgia where they use alternative medicine. So I went and received treatments for a year at $18,000 per month – it cost me everything. The cancer went into remission at the end of that year of treatments.

I had started attending a different church and I asked the Youth Pastor, "How do I grow in Jesus, how do I grow?" He advised me to get a good-sized yellow paper tablet and my Bible, and whenever the preacher is preaching, ask God to show you what highlights of the message to write down. Also write down all the scriptures that are referenced, then go home and go over it all and God will start revealing Himself to you.

I have to tell you…I started growing spiritually for the first time ever. I was saved on May 3, 1979. I was in 11th grade of school and I was so radically changed that one of my teachers called my mom and asked, "What in the world has happened to John because the temper is gone and he's like a totally different person." Well, my mom ended up giving the plan of salvation to my (atheist) teacher, and she received Christ.

I went for another blood test which showed the cancer was back in the blood, as well as finding chemicals in my blood that I had worked with on my job. I shared my circumstances with the Pastor and asked if he would pray with me. He said, "We don't just pray at this church, we lay hands on the sick and they will recover when we pray." That was the first time I had ever heard of that!

The pastor and others laid hands on me as they prayed for me. I went back to the doctor a month later and the cancer and chemicals were gone! God healed me! It baffled the doctors. I was shocked myself, but so happy because I certainly didn't want to go through all that again. It was absolutely incredible, and that's when I started learning about healing.

I had a real passion for the sick because I had been sick for a long time with incredible back-nerve pain that would shoot all the way down to my ankles. The shots hadn't been helping anymore, and I had to use the TENS unit for hours and hours a day. There were a lot of things I couldn't do anymore. I just needed relief from it.

I went to a healing meeting (conference), and it was the first time I had ever seen the glory of the Lord literally fill the place. But just before the glory of the Lord came, it was as though Jesus walked through the crowd. And I'm telling you...it was the most awesome fragrance of vanilla and cinnamon as He walked through the crowd, and the glory fell. I had never seen anything like that before; it resembled a really thick heavy cloud in the whole room.

There were about 250 people in that room but I could only see about 16 people through the cloud. Even the pastor was on his knees because he couldn't stand up. I prayed, "God, would you heal the discs in my back?" I was just in awe and I couldn't stand in the presence of the Lord. I felt an oily substance on my arms.

Nobody prayed for anyone in that room, but God DID heal my back, and I haven't had any problems or back pain in years! And not only my healing occurred, every person in that room was healed of whatever problems they were experiencing.

The pastor's planned service just stopped and we let the Holy Spirit do what He wanted to do. He healed people of inner torment, demons came out of people, people's legs and arms grew out, and so many other miraculous healings took place all while no other person touched any of them. It was just absolutely incredible! My back pain was gone, and I just worshipped God all the way home!

That experience caused me to get really hungry for God! I studied the Word and worshipped Him day and night for several days, because I had been in so much pain, taking many drugs to combat the pain, so I'm in awe of how God instantly healed me and the pain was gone!

At that time, I hadn't known anything about taking my authority, but now I do and I use it for His glory often. And God is still teaching me new things every day about healing and taking authority in His name.

Skin Cancer Healed

I was at a large church when a woman asked me to pray for her because she had extensive, advanced skin cancer.

I told her yes, and that I would be happy to pray for her.

I told her that God is the healer, not I, and then I prayed for her healing in Jesus' name.

She immediately began to feel heat in her skin and all the pain miraculously went away.

When I saw her again the next week, she had been to the Doctor the prior week after our prayer together, and the Doctor confirmed that the cancer was completely gone!

Praise the Lord, the healer!

Eyesight Restored

I saw a woman in a store who seemed to be having a problem reading the ingredients on the label of a can. She had glasses so thick it was like looking through the bottom of a bottle; she was considered legally blind.

I asked her if I could help her, and told her that I very often prayed for people. I then explained that God is the healer. I asked if she would like me to pray for her—she smiled and said, "Yes, please."

I put my hand on her arm and prayed for her eyesight to be restored. Then I asked if she could see any better and she said no. I told her I would pray again, and this time I commanded, in Jesus' name, for her to see. I then asked again, and she could see a little better. I prayed again—she said, "WOW, I feel really hot."

I told her that it was the Holy Spirit touching her and healing her. She said, "I can't see at all now, everything is very blurry." I told her to take off her glasses, and when she did she began weeping under the presence of God saying, "I can see clearly." She read me the can label, and then we praised God together, right there in the aisle of the store.

I asked her if she would like to receive Jesus Christ as her Savior, and she said, "Yes!" I then led her in prayer so she could receive Jesus Christ and be saved.

Even Trees Obey

My Grandfather, my dad's father, had given him a walnut tree when I was just a kid, and it was only about a 2-foot-tall twig when my dad planted it. When the tree was full-grown, it provided good shade over a swing that my dad had made. He loved to work in the garden with his flowers, and then he would swing and drink tea.

Unfortunately, now the whole top of that tree was dying and dad felt really bad about possibly losing the tree because it was something that his father had given him. So while we were sitting on that swing talking one day after I got home from work, I said to him, "Dad, it doesn't have to be that way." He asked, "What do you mean?" I said, "Well, this is your property, it's your tree, and you have the authority over this property." He agreed. Then I said, "But, we could both agree that this tree WILL live, and all this dead junk in the top of the tree would get out so new life could come, because you are giving me permission to pray over the tree."

He gave me permission to pray; we laid hands on that tree together, his hand first and then, as a son, I put my hand on top of his hand. We then commanded all the dead stuff to get out of that tree and for new life to come into the tree top and fill in the whole dead area. In the name of Jesus Christ, we commanded that tree to live!

This all happened just before a medical issue happened to my dad.

I came home one day from work, and my mom said that my dad, who was in his 80s, wasn't feeling well with a pain in his stomach. I called the doctor to find out what was going on, and the doctor recommended that I call an ambulance to take him to the hospital.

It was discovered that he was bleeding internally, but they couldn't determine where. So I prayed, and asked some friends to pray that the doctors would be able to find the source of the bleeding and be able to fix the problem.

After tests and scans, they found a two inch tear in his small intestine going into his large intestine that the doctors would be able to repair through surgery. They told us that had the tear been up higher, they wouldn't have been able to fix it because it requires a much more extensive surgery that they felt dad would not have been able to withstand.

They were successful in fixing the problem through surgery. He was given five pints of blood during surgery, and then he had to go to a rehab facility afterward. He was in rehab for 30 days, and while he was gone we had a horrendous thunder and rain storm with winds that blew like

Dixie! It took me over an hour to pick up all the sticks and dead junk that had fallen out of that walnut tree.

I told my dad about it, and that God was growing that tree. He said, "You're kidding!" "No, I'm not Dad, God's growing that tree," I said. Every day my Mom and I visited him, and I would tell him about the tree growing new shoots in the top of the tree. And do you know…when he returned home after those 30 days in rehab, he stood on the patio looking up at that tree and just cried (and I mean cried!). Tears were just flowing…happy tears!

He was in awe that God took all that dead junk out of that tree, and new life was growing. Most of the new branches had grown 2 feet tall, had leaves already, and were filling in that whole dead area. He could hardly believe it, and said, "We got what we prayed for. We got what we asked for." He was just beside himself. And that tree totally filled in, and my dad was just in awe that God did that for him after we prayed and asked Him to.

There are a lot of things, it says in John 15:7, that if we abide in God (abide means to stay), and if we stay in God and God stays in us, we can ask whatever we want and God said He'll do it. Well, we did with that tree. We stood on that scripture verse. And God literally took all the dead stuff out during the storm, and gave all new life within 30 days.

We gave God all the praise and glory for it. I was so glad that my dad was able to see that awesome miracle before leaving his earthly home.

Praying in the Spirit

A couple years ago I went to a 4-day conference where a lot of people attended from many other states. Multiple speakers spoke and taught us new ways of how we could pray in the Spirit (tongues), starting with a different letter of the alphabet. It sounded a bit like speaking in Chinese, or French, or Italian, just by starting out with a different syllable.

There were people in the crowd who were actually hearing the plan of salvation in their own language! I just thank God for teaching us all of that.

Conference Miracles

At that same conference, I had compassion because of all the sicknesses that I had been through. When I see people who are sick, some in wheel chairs, God will literally highlight those people to me.

This day, God highlighted a guy who was in a motorized wheelchair that he operated with a couple fingers. And I started talking to he and his wife before the conference began, and he told me that he was going to the conference and then to a family reunion. He had been given a diagnosis of dying within the month because he had ALS (Amytrophic Lateral Sclerosis, also known as Lou Gehrig's disease).

As he was telling me about all this, a faith arose in me and I asked, "Would you mind if I prayed for you?" He answered, "Sure!" So I asked God how to pray for this man, and I prayed in the Spirit for about an hour before the service. I told him that God highlighted him to me for a reason, and I personally believe we are going to see you get out of this wheelchair this week, and that's what I'm believing God for. I told him I wanted to pray for him again after the service; he and his wife totally agreed that they would love it if I prayed for them again.

After the service which included many miracles, signs, and wonders, I started praying for that man again. God led other people to come stand with us in prayer as well.

There's one thing I've learned about spiritual healings—it's great to pray in English, and it's great to pray in the Spirit, but then there is also a relationship with Jesus. In a relationship, you have to stop and listen for the Holy Spirit to talk to you as well. Otherwise it's a one-way street where you're doing all the talking but you're not hearing the Holy Spirit talk to you and give you direction.

I stopped praying and heard this little voice tell me to get him up out of that wheelchair and stand him up. I told the man, "God said to stand you up.

Personal Testimonials

I'll hang onto you." So I literally stood the man up and commanded him to walk in Jesus' name. He was very unsteady, but another guy helped me, and the man walked eight steps. It took a lot to get his legs moving, but God allowed him to walk eight steps before he sat back down in his chair.

We all praised and worshipped Jesus for those eight steps, which he hadn't been able to walk in over a month. He had been working when this affliction came on him, and from the time he started having trouble walking and his motor skills were affected, it was only 3-4 weeks before he was in that wheelchair. The doctors told him that his was a very aggressive kind of ALS, and that typically people will die within two months of getting the disease.

I told this man, "Granted, the doctors are the doctors...but...Jesus can and will intervene. Satan comes to kill, steal, and destroy, but God comes to give us life and life more abundantly. I'd like to pray for you every day." He and all the others whom God had put around him agreed.

This man's wife generally put him to bed using a mini-crane device that picks him up out of the chair and gets him onto the bed. So that night she used it and got him to bed.

The next morning he woke and exclaimed, "God, I feel strength in my body that I haven't had. So he started thanking God for giving him strength. That man got up out of bed, took his walker and started walking all through the house, praising Jesus that he could walk! He praised Jesus that he didn't have ALS any longer. The more he praised and thanked Jesus, the more strength he got.

The Bible tells us that the joy of the Lord gives us strength. He was so happy! When his wife woke up and reached for him to tell him Good Morning, like she always did, and found him not there, she got up very concerned, especially when she saw the wheelchair still sitting next to their bed.

He told her that God woke him up at 4:00 a.m. and that he had been up walking through the house since then. And he said that every time he would make a whole pass through the house, he got stronger.

That day he came to the meeting...not in his wheelchair...with his walker!

It was so exciting! We all praised God for that, and we prayed over him again for life to come into every cell, and for ALS to leave his body in the name of Jesus Christ. He just kept feeling stronger.

After the service, we walked all around praising and worshipping, thanking God for this miracle we were all witnessing.

The next morning, he woke up and said he felt extremely good, so he left his walker and walked all through the house all day with only a cane.

Personal Testimonials

And the more he walked and praised God, the stronger he got!

When he came back to the meeting that evening, he said to me, "John, I was coming to this meeting, hoping to be healed, and God healed my body! I feel so good, that I called my boss this morning and they are giving me my job back. I was going to go to this 4-day conference, and then go see family at our reunion, hopefully lead a bunch of my family members to the Lord, and then die. But now I'm going to go to the family and give a praise report of what Jesus has done for me. I hope they get saved! And I'm going back to work. Glory to God, He healed me! He healed me, God healed me!"

He gave his testimony that night which, of course, encouraged everybody! No matter what kind of death sentence you are given, God is more than able to heal your body, heal your mind, heal your soul, and prosper you as His word promises.

Also, at that same 4-day conference, I was driving a diesel pickup truck at the time, and a round-trip was about 40 miles. I had money in my wallet that I was going to use for gas that evening, but the Lord instructed me to give it all in the offering. I said, "That's all the money I have, Father, for fuel for my truck." The Lord responded, "Do you trust me?" "Yes, I trust you," I answered. He said, "Then give it." "But God, I don't have any fuel, so I won't be able to drive back and forth to the conference." The Lord reiterated, "Do you trust me?" "Yes, I do" I again answered. "Then trust and obey," the Lord told me.

So...out of faith I did obey and gave all that money in the offering, and I didn't get paid again for two weeks. I just kept praying over the truck that the gas would multiply. I drove that truck back and forth for four days when the needles on both gas tanks were way under 'E'. I knew that running a diesel out of fuel was a bad thing, but miraculously it did not run out of fuel! Every time I made it back home I was just thanking and praising God that I could trust Him.

Isn't it just like our flesh to have a tendency to not trust Him in all things? Well, unfortunately the next day I got in fear and asked a friend to loan me $20 for fuel. And then I repented of it afterward because God was trying to teach me that I can always trust Him. But we don't always have the faith that we need, and that is what forgiveness is for. I repented of it and God has given me other chances to obey when He instructs me to do something, to give money, or time, physical belongs, or whatever it is.

The Lord blessed me, despite my lack of faith in that instance.

At that conference, I saw God move in another way that I had never witnessed before. The Evangelist gave a Word of Knowledge that ladies should use their compacts with a mirror to look

Personal Testimonials

into each other's mouths, and he released words to those who needed a miracle in their mouths that gold crowns would miraculously appear. We literally watched the physical move of God on people. For one woman, it started with a few specks of gold literally dancing on top of her silver amalgam fillings. Within a 24-hour period, God had replaced the silver amalgam fillings in 20+ teeth with gold crowns and gold fillings in her whole mouth. And there were no tool marks on any of that gold.

It was truly incredible, and with that we give all the praise, honor, and the glory to Jesus!

Hernia Healed

I talked to a fella who had a hernia near his belly button. His warehouse job involved him throwing a lot of boxes above his head. He told me that the pain was getting really intense because the hernia was getting fired up because of all the hard work he was doing.

I told him, "I am a Christian, and I pray for people. I would like to pray for you if that's ok." He said, "Sure!"

So I laid hands on him and prayed that the hernia would be healed in the name of Jesus Christ. Instantly the pain went away. He said he felt a burning sensation in his stomach as Jesus healed him!

He hasn't had any more hernia problems since then.

We give all the praise and glory to God that He healed that guy of that hernia.

College Mission

One day God sent me out of town, about an hour from my home, to a city where there is a big college. I had no idea why I was going there, but I just obeyed God and went.

I had never been on that campus before, so I found the administration office and the Lord gave me a name when I pulled up in front of the office. I thought I was there to pray for a lady who had just been diagnosed with cancer. I don't always get it right, but I walked in and there was only one girl in the office. I asked her if the lady, with the name given me from the Lord, worked there, and she said, "No, why?" I said, "Well, the Lord sent me here from where I live, an hour away, and told me to pray for that lady. I don't get it right every time, but I think she has breast cancer, and I am to lay hands on her and God will heal her." And she said, "No, there is no one here by that name, but I think you're here because of me." "Why is that," I asked. She said, "Because I'm a 'new' Christian and I've been struggling with God about healing. I don't know anyone who prays for healing, and I've been talking to God about it."

So I was there maybe 15 minutes, just sharing some testimonies like I'm sharing with you, and the Lord just opened the door right into that girl's heart so she knew without a doubt that she was the reason I was there. And I knew too, even after talking with her for just a few minutes, that God set us up and worked it all out.

That lady was young, probably in her 20s, and she just opened her heart up to God. I prayed with her and the Lord went in and healed some heart issues. I encouraged her to step out in faith when she hears God speak to her and then radically obey, and He WILL speak to her. It was just incredible watching what all God did for that girl in 15 minutes.

I didn't want to keep her from her work too long, but she was totally blessed when I walked out of there. She thanked me for obeying, and after leaving there I had an incredible time with God.

When you're serving the Lord, there is just nothing better, in Jesus' name!

Knee Repaired in a Store

Some time ago at the church I was attending, a group of 20-30 of us got together on a week night, to go on 'treasure hunts'—basically, we would pray in the Holy Spirit and ask God to give us clues as to who He wants us to go out and find in public. For example, He may have us look for someone with a red shirt, maybe a certain type of pants, they might look a certain way, or by signs literally in businesses. So we would hunt those people down, and then God would give us words of knowledge and tell us specific things about that person that they hadn't told anyone. Those words of knowledge opens a door to witness to them, encourage them, and if they need healing in their body, we pray for them and watch God heal them.

We start by pairing up older persons with younger persons; not necessarily because of age, but basically we paired people who knew how to pray for people and give words of knowledge, with those who wanted to learn.

This particular night I was paired with a 16 or 17-year-old young man. God directed us to a store and had us looking for a person in a wheelchair or one of those motorized scooters with a basket in the front that the store makes available for people who have difficulty walking.

We found a mother and a daughter in an aisle, and the mother was using one of the store's motorized scooters. The young man with me got all excited because that scooter was on our list, along with the person being a woman with left leg problems.

As it turned out, she had torn her meniscus on the inside of her left knee and her kneecap was out of joint, causing extreme pain and difficulty walking. She had her leg in a brace for stability because she could hardly get from her car seat onto the scooter without her daughter's help. We spoke to the woman and she agreed that she would like to have us pray for her. And the daughter was somewhat enthralled with my young friend because he was a nice looking kid.

I coached the boy to ask the Lord how we should pray for the mother. He took a moment, and then said that the Lord told him to pray for her, but that she needed to take off that brace first. So she did take it off. He then lightly touched the top of her knee and prayed that God would repair the meniscus and realign her knee. Immediately the knee pain went away and the kneecap popped as it literally went back into place. He felt it, as did she, and he wasn't moving his hand at all.

They were both in awe...actually shocked was more like it...for what God had just done. She had extreme heat come into that leg, and then within about 10 minutes, all the pain in her whole leg went away. She stood on it, she cried, and it was just incredible.

About a month before this encounter, the young man had attended a church camp where a bunch of teenagers were learning how to operate in the gifts of the Spirit, including prayers for healing.

Towards the middle of that week, he prayed, "God, I'm really short for my age and my grade. I want to be three inches taller." So, you know how kids are...they were playing around and whatnot, and they prayed for him to grow three inches. First they commanded one leg to grow and it grew out three inches. Then they commanded the other leg to grow four inches, and it did! Then all the kids got up and ran away.

The boy got up and was having trouble walking and was falling down. He called out "Guys, guys...don't leave me like this." They came back and were all laughing, you know how kids are. They prayed again for the one leg to shorten by that extra inch, which it amazingly did. So both legs were now three inches longer, and his pants were too short...they call them 'floods'. His mother wasn't thrilled about having to buy him all new pants.

The young man was sharing that testimony story with that woman and her daughter (who was about the same age as the boy). The daughter said, "I want that too because I'm short for my age." Her mom shook her head 'yes' in agreement. I told him, "Go ahead, pray for her!" So he reached down, touched the girl's ankles, and she literally grew three inches taller right there in the aisle of that store. She began hooting and hollering and carrying on, which, unfortunately, got the attention of some of the store staff.

They came and watched us for a little bit. As soon as we were through praying for that mother and daughter, and they were both blessed and in awe of what God had done in their lives, the young man and I started to leave to find someone else to whom the Lord wanted us to minister. The store staff came up to us and told us that we couldn't pray for people and, basically, we couldn't perform miracles in that store. They said we had to leave now, and escorted us out of the store.

I said, "Praise God, we got thrown out of the store for doing what God told us to do." We had quite a testimony that evening of what God did, and of being tossed out of the store; not a bad thing, it was a good thing. Eventually we went back and did it again.

The thing was that God led us to the right people, and He really moved. I gave them the words of knowledge of which only they knew, and encouraged them spiritually. They were forever changed, and so were we.

Personal Testimonials

Healing Lunch

I was in a popular local store that's where I enjoy having lunch and coffee before I shop.

As I was eating, I noticed a woman with her son at another table. She was eating but the son had his head down on his arms lying on the table. I could tell he didn't feel well because I don't know of any child that wouldn't be eating the good food the store offered. So I asked the woman if her son was sick. She said he had a really bad headache, so I asked her if I could pray for him. With smiles, they both said yes.

I approached them and knelt next to the boy. I asked him if I could touch him on the head. He said yes, so I put my hand on his head and commanded the pain, vision impairment, and headache to go in Jesus' name.

I asked the boy how he was feeling, and he said his head was tingling, so he laid his head back down on the table.

His mom thanked me, and then I shared with her how my God, Jesus Christ, went about healing all sorts of sicknesses, and that He told us through scripture that we can do what He did, and more!

I then went back to my table and finished my lunch. About 10 minutes later I noticed the little boy was feeling much better—laughing and eating and talking to his mom. I commented to her that he appeared to be feeling better, and she said he started feeling better shortly after I prayed. They both thanked me again. I told her that she needed to thank Jesus Christ, as He is the healer.

She said, "Thank you Jesus for healing my son." Then I left.

Since that experience, I have encountered that woman and her son in that store three times. When she sees me, she always stops approximately 12 feet away and yells, "John! Thank you for praying for my son, and thank You Jesus for healing my son!", as many other shoppers heard her and turn to look at them and me.

Isn't God Good!?

Medication Miracle

I went to a small group from my church, and among our group was a small team planning a trip to Africa soon to be a blessing at an orphanage and to some of the missionaries there.

The team was allowed to bring only two large suitcases containing medications to administer to anyone who needed them.

As we were talking about the trip plans, Jesus prompted me to ask the team: "Would you be in agreement with me that when you get to Africa and put the medications on the shelves, Jesus would multiply what was given?" They all agreed. So I asked God how He wanted me to pray; then I prayed as God told me.

When the team returned from Africa, the team leader told me that as the nurse put the medications on the shelves, Jesus *did multiply them*, and they were able to add six more shelves for a total of eight.

WOW, what an awesome God we serve! We give all praises to You, King Jesus, for all You did. Your miracles also build our faith for more!

Bye-Bye Demons!

I attended a 2-hour conference where they were speaking on casting demons out of people. They also said that sometimes demons will physically show up on a person, like in a little bit of a red spot the size of a quarter, and they can move around in the body.

One Saturday morning my dad came and woke me up and said that mom was in really bad pain. It was in her right kidney, and the pain was severe. I had never seen my mother, or anyone else, in that much pain. She decided she needed to go to the hospital, and we agreed. We took her by car because she didn't want to go by ambulance.

The doctors performed a bunch of tests but couldn't find anything wrong that would be causing that pain. They gave her a hefty shot of morphine, and she just sat there rocking back and forth in absolutely horrific pain. My father went out to talk to the Doctors, who seemed to be just be chat-chatting, and he told them, "If you don't do something for my wife, I'm taking her out of this hospital and taking her to a different hospital... do you hear me?"

The doctors said they couldn't give her any more pain medicine and that they don't know what's wrong with her. My dad went back into the room, and all of a sudden the pain stopped in the

Personal Testimonials

kidney, and it moved to her stomach. The doctor said, "Well, whatever that is, it's not going to kill her because it moved."

When he said that, and with the pain moving like it did, I was reminded of what I had learned just the night before at that conference. Everyone else was out of the room with just a curtain between the beds, and I told him, "Dad, I think I know what this is...will you agree with me in prayer?" He said, "Absolutely!"

I told dad to put his hand on mom's shoulder, and I put my hand on her other shoulder, and he gave me permission (because he's the head of the house) to pray over mom. And I commanded that demon to get out of her right now in the name of Jesus! I'm telling you...it was like a switch was flipped; all the pain went away! She laid down and just rested for not even an hour.

Now, if you've ever had morphine, you know that typically you will be 'out of it' for the whole day because it's a powerful drug. But, within the hour she was up and ready to go. They released her with no more pain or problems.

Both Mom and Dad were baffled. Like, where did this thing come from? I have learned from my walk with God that you have to be very careful of what you buy on vacation, or from stores, or whatever. I don't care what it is, especially a thrift store where other people have owned things, because we don't know what's been prayed over them or curses that have been put on those items. The closer I've gotten to God, the more the Lord has shown me that even Christians, including myself, can have things in our possessions that aren't Godly.

I went home, prayed, and fasted, and asked God where in the heck did this demon come from that's harassing my mom. Even though she never had that problem again, I said, "We need to do a house cleaning." And that involved strong prayers over our home. My parents were Baptist and I was non-denominational, so I told them to pray in English and I'll pray in the Spirit.

I began in the attic and literally anointed every door and every window in our whole house, including the basement and garage. In every room and space I went into, I bound any demons that were in the house and commanded them to shut up and follow me. And after I anointed every place in the house, and pleaded the blood of Jesus over our home, I opened the front door and commanded every demon to leave our house! We never had another issue like that with my mother.

And then a few weeks later, my dad, who was in his 80s, was carrying two arms full of groceries down to the freezer in the basement, and the same thing! He tripped and fell half-way down, head-over-heels to the bottom of the stairs and landed in my tools. I wasn't home when this happened, but to our surprise he wasn't hurt in any way. He wasn't

Personal Testimonials

sore, no black-and-blue bruises, or anything. I personally believe that an angel caught him (my own take on things).

Dad said, "What the heck's going on? We did a house-cleaning." I said, "I don't know, but we're going to get to the bottom of it." So I fasted and prayed about it, and asked God to show me what in the world was going on. And God started to show me things.

When I was on a Caribbean cruise, I brought home a small souvenir of this guy on a donkey and a jug in his hand, and God told me that the person who made that is into witchcraft. I asked, "Why hasn't it bothered us for 10 years, why now?" God replied, "The closer you get to Me, stuff starts to manifest." So I pleaded the blood of Jesus over that thing, then busted it up and threw it in the trash can. And the incidences stopped.

Over the course of the next several months, God started showing me more things, more things, more things. I was in sales for a long time, and a customer asked if I would like to have some handmade fine-needle work pieces. They were extremely awesome and looked like paintings, but they were made with thread. I took four of them and brought them home. It wasn't until two years later that the Lord told me to get rid of them...get them out of the house...because my finances had majorly fell after I brought those into my home. As I sought the Lord and asked why this was happening, He said there is poverty connected to the paintings. I asked what I should do with them, and He told me to bust them up, pray the blood of Jesus over them, and throw them away. I did… immediately!

And God showed me that even a horse shoe looks innocent, but people claim them as being lucky. But Christianity is not luck; it's relationship. And I got rid of every single thing that God showed me, and as I did, we all started getting healthier. It was quite amazing actually.

I just want to tell you to be careful what you buy. Statues and especially things like masks that look like people's faces. There is a lot of witchcraft connected to things, like 'lucky elephants', rabbit's foot, and all that type of junk. I don't want any witchcraft in my house at all. You also have to be careful what you watch, what you hear, and where you go because you can, unknowingly, pick up junk and bring it home.

Personal Testimonials

Tongue-Tie Healing

One Sunday, a friend's sister came to our church, and after the service we were talking. She told me of a problem she was having with her tongue. She was born with an affliction of being tongue-tie (ankyloglossia), caused by a web of tissue (lingual frenulum) that attaches the underside of the tongue to the floor of the mouth. This caused her to not be able to speak properly.

I told her that God heals, and she agreed that she knows He does. I asked if she would like me to pray for her to be healed by Jesus. I shared a couple healing testimonies to bring her faith up to believe that she could receive that healing.

I then prayed over her, and afterwards I said, "People don't always feel something right away, but do you feel anything?" She said, "Yes, I feel like something is messing with the underside of my tongue, and I feel extreme heat in my mouth." I told her, "That is the presence of God going to work healing your tongue."

Within about 10-15 minutes of us praying, she said, "Wow, it is 100% better than it was." She was speaking just as clear as if she never had that problem. She said, "Thank you." I replied, "No, you need to thank Jesus! He's the one who healed you. Give Him all the praise, honor and glory for it."

She started thanking and praising God for it, in that she was freed from that tongue-tie affliction.

Personal Testimonials

Dead Battery Challenge

One day one of my friends called me and told me that he had gone somewhere, and now he's ready to return home but his jeep won't start. I asked whether he had prayed for the jeep to start...no, he hadn't. So I told him, "Well, pray that it will start."

He did pray, but it still didn't start. He asked me to come to his location, quite a few miles away, to help him jump-start his vehicle. So I did go to see if I could help him.

When I got there, he had the hood open and was checking for the possible cause of the problem. He said the battery cables were tight, but when he turned the key there wasn't even a click. I told him that I did have jumper cables, but I would like to pray over it first. So I just prayed in the spirit a little bit over that jeep, and then commanded, in Jesus' name, that it start and keep running until we could get it to an auto repair shop to get diagnostic testing done.

As I was commanding it to start, to his surprise, it started right up! I wasn't surprised at all.

So I followed him to an AutoZone. One of the employees tested it and told my friend, "Man, you're lucky to have gotten this vehicle started because there is nothing left in this battery at all.

It's totally dead!" Then he said, "I don't know how it even stayed running to get here." I responded, "Oh, Jesus did that....we asked Him to, and He did it!"

We had a nice conversation with that young man, and he was in awe over what had happened. My friend asked me, "Why did it start for you but not for me?" I said I didn't know why not—it's always up to God to decide these things.

The whole episode turned into a nice evening. My friend took me out to dinner and had great conversation together. And I'm confident that the young man at AutoZone had a lot to think about after witnessing what God had done that night too.

Personal Testimonials

Faulty Brakes

I used to be in sales, and I drove a lot! Between 1200 and 1400 miles a week. I was paying off doctor bills as fast as I could, but money was very tight because the amounts I was paying was like having to pay a triple mortgage to get those medical bills paid off.

I carried a lot of product samples in my car, which was a lot of weight. My brakes sounded like metal-on-metal grinding terribly, which was not a good thing. I prayed, "God, right now I don't have the finances to put new brakes on this car." And then I commanded in the name of Jesus Christ that new brake pads grow out on this car! I repeated that command three times, and then the grinding stopped.

I had forgotten about the brakes after that, until I went to have a tire fixed that I had punctured running over a nail. They advised me that I was due for a tire rotation, so they did the rotation too. Then I asked the repairman, "Hey, do you mind if I go out there and take a look at my brakes to see what shape the pads are on there?" He said, "Sure, go ahead and look."

Wouldn't you know it...God is so good! It was as though I had brand new brake pads! I had never changed them after praying for them to grow out, and they weren't grinding with that metal-on-metal sound at all either. Because of the amazing miracle Jesus gave me, those brakes lasted on that car until I sold it nearly three years later!

Rapid Weight Loss

Eight years ago, I was invited to a small home church in Northern Michigan. I wanted to see their awesome log house next to a trout stream. WOW, it was beautiful. The salmon go up that stream to spawn—it was incredible to witness as we were worshipping.

God told the host to approach me and pray for supernatural weight loss. I said, "Yes, please do. I have tried everything to lose weight." He prayed—I felt nothing, but I thanked Jesus nonetheless.

Approximately two weeks went by when I noticed that my pants were loose. I got on the scale and discovered that I had lost 10 pounds and two pant sizes. Within the next eight months, I lost 110 pounds. Praise the Lord!

I started praying for other people to lose weight. Some lost weight as I prayed, and some took longer but they did lose weight. I would tell the people to hold onto their skirts and pants, just in case, and almost all obeyed.

I think God has a great sense of humor, and that He was laughing so hard that tears were flowing.

We prayed for one woman who needed to lose a good amount of weight. She didn't heed our advice to hold onto her skirt, and she didn't receive the weight loss on the spot. I told her that I was not the healer, God is! I encouraged her, again, to hold onto her skirt as she walked out the door. I quipped that this was going to be embarrassing.

As she got to her car and took her keys out of her purse to open the door, she lost her skirt, which she quickly pulled up as she looked around somewhat embarrassed.

She later told us that by the time she drove home and got on the scale, she had lost 80 pounds! She cried and praised God all night.

God is so good to us!

Personal Testimonials

Dad's Stroke - Seizures

I believe that seizures are caused by a demon that harasses a person's mind.

My father had a major stroke which affected the left side of his body and his mind. So I would bring him to work with me during that time when I was doing a lot of work for missionaries, widows, and divorced women with children. I would fix up their houses, fix up their rooms, and cut wood for them. Generally, whatever they needed to help them live better.

My father used to be a welder and pipe fitter, but could no longer do much of anything after his stroke. But over time, he regained his strength and abilities to work again, except for a bit of his memory; he couldn't remember certain things, but everything else—his whole body—came back to health. I would bring him on jobs and show him how to solder something, get him started, and then watch him do it. The first time was great and he could do it! It was incredible what God did for him.

My parents were awesome Christian people. However, the church they attended had never taught them anything about healing and the miracles that God's disciples did in the Bible's book of Acts. They had been taught that those things in the New Testament had all stopped. Well...they didn't stop.

One night we were all watching TV; I was on the couch, and mom and dad sat rocking together, holding hands, and were enjoying popcorn as they often do. All of a sudden dad started having a seizure. I jumped up off that couch, put my hand on his chest, and commanded, "You come out of him right now in the name of Jesus! Get out in Jesus' name!" It instantly left, and never came back! Our house was in peace without any further problems for them at all! It was just incredible.

My dad typically went to bed around 10:00 p.m. and my mom would go to bed around 11:00 p.m.. But while I was attending the healing conferences, they would stay up until 1:00 a.m. waiting for me to come home so I could tell them all about what God had done there. I would share the experiences for about an hour or so, and then we would all go to bed.

I told them, "Instead of you waiting up for me to come home, why don't you just come with me?" So they did. They started seeing miracles happen at the church, and my dad said, "This is just totally wrong, John, to not have seen any miracles like this until we're in our 80s, and then see all these miracles! It shouldn't be that way." I replied, "No, it shouldn't. But I'm just learning too."

My parents were able to experience several personal hands-on miracles before they left this place. They were just in awe of what God had done.

Personal Testimonials

Be Careful Who Your Friends Are Because You May Become Like Them

I was friends with a couple at the church I attended who were the parents of a 14-year-old boy. This kid was hanging around with some 'bad' kids at school, and they had been experimenting with different drugs trying to get high. The kid really didn't have a clue about anything. One day he went to his grandparent's home and took pills from their medicine cabinet. What he didn't know is that some were uppers and some were downers, but they were medically prescribed for different medical conditions.

One night at home, he took a whole handful of some of those pills thinking he was going to get high. The whole family was watching TV and eating popcorn in the dark when his younger sister (7-8 at the time) remarked that her brother's lips looked blue. She started making a fuss about that, and the parents thought she was just messing around (they had several children), but the sister insisted saying, "No, his lips look blue!"

So Dad turned on the lights, and to his horror, his lips were blue alright, but he wasn't breathing. So Dad threw the boy onto the floor, called 911, and the emergency attendant talked him through doing CPR over the phone. The emergency crew took him by ambulance to the hospital. Doctors pumped his stomach and did a drug test to see what was in his system. The kid slipped into a coma. It looked like he was just laying there sleeping. He was breathing on his own without needing oxygen, but he just didn't wake up.

The Mom called me and a friend of mine who had previously ministered with me, and asked us to come and pray for her son. So we went to the hospital and, while waiting in the waiting room, I was talking to the Lord about it, asking Him how we should pray for this boy.

The doctors were telling the parents the worst scenario; of course they have to. If he does wake up, he will probably be brain dead or be a vegetable the rest of his life because of what he took. His kidneys are damaged, liver is damaged, and the list went on and on.

After they finished talking to the doctors, I told my friends, "Do not listen to what the doctors are saying, just listen to what Jesus says! Jesus says that by His stripes we *ARE* already healed. We need to stand on God's word!"

And then God told me that I needed to talk to the boy's father alone. So I took him out to the waiting room and told him that he needed to intercede for his son and renounce the way the boy had allowed the spirit of death to come into him. I asked if he would be willing to do that, and he said, yes! So he prayed and asked God to forgive his son for allowing the spirit of death to come into him because of the drugs.

He did that, and we went back into the room. Then we prayed for that boy that absolutely nothing would be wrong with him. We spoke life over every organ in his body and over his mind—we just spoke to the mountain!

We were in the ICU and the nurses were in there working, talking to us a little bit. We had just done what the Holy Spirit had told us to do. We sang a little praise and worship to God all A cappella, and we all prayed in the spirit over that boy (mom, dad, friend and I).

And you know...the boy was stone cold like he was dead already. His flesh was cold and his skin was grayish. I've never seen that before, but as we were praying over him and ministering to his family, all of a sudden we saw one ear...just one ear...began turning pink. He was covered with a blanket, but his arms were exposed and they were stone cold, as well as his face. We pulled the blanket down a little and even his chest was cold. I'm thinking, what the heck...and he's almost dead, and they weren't sure if he would ever wake up from it.

I commanded, "You WILL wake up in the name of Jesus, and there will be nothing wrong with you!" My friend spoke to him as well, and suddenly his right ear also began turning pink.

Even the nurse said, "That doesn't happen." So she was in awe too, and then we watched both ears turn completely pink, and then his face! When his face turned pink, it was warm to the touch. Within about 30 minutes, we witnessed that healing going all the way through that boy's body. We turned the lights on, and the nurses and all of us watched the miracle happening before our eyes!

All I can say is that God was on that boy! The nurse called the doctor, and he was very encouraged to see what was happening, especially that the warmth was coming back into his body. They couldn't explain it, other than God! God got the glory for it all.

The next day I called to find out how he was doing. His condition was the same, still 'out of it'. But on the 3rd day...which is kind of interesting...the 3rd day that boy woke up, talked, and there was absolutely nothing wrong with him. The doctors and nurses all said it was a miracle! We know it was a miracle because he went from almost dead to literally nothing wrong with him. They could not find anything wrong with that kid!

I got a phone call from the boy's mom about 3-4 days after that. The boy was back home but was not sleeping well, and was being tormented. The mom asked if I would come and talk to him. I said sure, and took off to see him.

I met with extreme warfare before I could get to the house...and I mean extreme! I could

Personal Testimonials

physically feel the devil fighting against me. But I fought through that with God's glory and we won! I drove into that driveway and went and talked to the boy. I asked him, "What's the problem?"

He didn't really want his mom there to hear our conversation, but finally I told him that his mom needed to hear all this too because this whole situation has been extremely difficult for his mother and father. There were no other siblings around and he said, "I was in hell...literally, I was in hell while I was out of it. I need Jesus! I don't want to go back to that place. He said, I don't want to go to hell, I want to go to Heaven with Jesus, but not before it's time. He repented of getting into drugs and hanging around with the wrong people. He asked God to forgive him of his sins and he accepted Jesus Christ as his personal Savior that day. And I'm telling you...it was like night and day difference in that kid. He wanted to grow in the Lord.

So we got him a Bible and he literally started reading it, which is amazing for a young kid. I asked him, "Who taught you about all these drugs and stuff?" He said some kids at school, and then there was a guy who was his dad's friend who used to come over to the house. The 'friend', who claimed to be a Christian, and the boy's dad were smoking weed in the silo and the kids caught them. The kids were totally ticked off, and I don't blame them. This is where the door to the evil had been opened; this was a generational problem.

So we prayed and broke that off from that family, and the dad repented.

When the dad confronted his friend about it, the friend claimed that he can hear the Holy Spirit talking better when he smokes dope—a lie from the pit of hell. When you're mind is altered, and you can't think straight, you are in the devil's playground. I told the dad, "That guy is not your friend. He's going to take you down the drain... he's taking your kid down the drain already. Your kid could have died or ended up maimed from what he did." The dad said, "Yes, I know it."

That started the family on a whole new walk with Jesus. The dad opened the door and the kids were following in his footsteps, but he didn't even realize what he had done. The kid thought he was just going to get high, but it almost killed him by taking that large mixture of drugs.

Now, they are a whole different family than they used to be. They are an awesome loving and caring family.

When anybody says that they can hear God more clearly when they smoke weed, they open themselves wide open to the devil to come on in, to kill, steal and destroy from them, or take their life. And if you're not saved, you're going to hell. There are two places when you leave this earth. If you have a personal relationship with Jesus Christ, you're going to heaven. If you don't, you're going to hell, it's that simple.

The Bible says to choose life...choose life!

Personal Testimonials

Miraculous Healings

One sunny Sunday afternoon I was at a park next to a beautiful lake enjoying watching all the people when I noticed a couple playing croquet with their family.

The woman was limping and used a cane, so I prayed to myself asking the Holy Spirit how I should pray for her. I then got up, approached her, and said, "Hello, how are you doing?" She said, "Great, we just got out of church and are playing a game before having lunch." I asked her what happened to her foot. She told me she had broken her foot a while ago, but it had never healed right and it was very painful.

Her husband walked over and I greeted him. I told them that God highlighted her to me and that I pray for people and then God heals them. I asked if she would like me to pray for her. Very happily, she said, "Yes, please do." Her husband held her hand and I bent down and touched her foot and commanded the pain to leave.

She said her foot was hot and tingling, so I stood up and told her, "Jesus is healing your foot." I then told her to try it out; she took my arm, gave her cane to her husband, and we walked five feet. She said it still hurt, so I touched her foot again asking Jesus if I missed anything. He said I did, and then He told me what to pray: "I command all pain and trauma to her foot, all tendons, ligaments, and the bone to straighten. In Jesus' name be healed." I suggested we walk more, and then she told us that *all the pain was gone*. She stopped, stood on her toes, and spun around. She said, "WOW, Jesus healed me!" She then started jumping up and down as she declared she had no pain and thanked Jesus for healing her.

Then she turned to me and said, "Thank you so much for being brave and stepping out to pray for me." She gave me a big hug.

Her husband shook my hand, and when he did God said to me he has a problem with his prostate; it was congested and inflamed. I said sir, this is what God just showed me, and I mentioned the prostate problems. He looked shocked and said he was having problems and had an appointment the next Monday with an Urologist. He asked me to pray for him; I did, and he then felt heat in his body, and then cooling tears were flowing. All three of us could feel God's presence on us so strongly. They both commented: "That feels so good, what is that?" I told them it was God's presence. Jesus healed them both and they felt His presence very strongly that day.

I prayed and asked God to show them that a deeper relationship is available to them by spending time with Jesus and seeking Him.

Those people were truly blessed, and so was I. As I walked away, the Holy Spirit said to me, "Good job. I love you son." I was weeping, thanking God for using me.

> *"You did not choose me, but I chose you and appointed you that you should go bear fruit, and your fruit should remain, that whatever you ask the father in my name he may give you."*
>
> — *John 15:16*

Knee Problem

A friend called me the other day and said he had been experiencing knee problems. He said that as he walks along, the knee would simply 'give out', and that it felt weak.

I told him, "This is what you say, 'I take my authority in Jesus Christ, and I command this knee to strengthen, I command the pain in this knee to leave in the name of Jesus Christ, and I command total healing to this knee. I drive out the demon that is afflicting this knee; I drive it out with the name and blood of Jesus'."

After he prayed that prayer, his knee was healed instantly.

Praise and glory in Jesus' name!

Personal Testimonials

More Than Enough God

Years ago I attended a mega church with approximately 15,000 people attending each weekend. We were hosting a Halloween 'Trunk-or-Treat' event in the church as an outreach to the community. Many of us personally donated candy, but I was also successful in getting a couple pallets of candy donated from a friend's business. I brought all that candy to the church and helped put it away. Then the evening of the event we prayed over everything and that people would get touched by God, get saved, and that the kids would have a great time.

Along with all the candy, someone had donated about 150 popcorn balls to be given out. A lot more children attended this event than we had anticipated, and our candy and popcorn ball supply was getting low. Some helpers came into the room where I was bagging up candy to convey their concerns of running out.

I said, "Well, what did Jesus do with the two loaves and five fishes? Jesus prayed and God multiplied them! So let's pray over the candy and popcorn balls, and then continue to give as though we had truckloads. Go ahead and give them generous handfuls!" So we all held hands and prayed over it all. Then I told them that I wanted to go out and bless the kids as well, so I took a large grocery sack full of candy and started blessing these kids by giving them handfuls of candy.

It was amazing…as we gave out popcorn balls, we always had more to hand out! We never ran out of those popcorn balls or candy! And the more amazing thing was that, at the end of the event, we ended up with so much candy that we gave it out to other church kids groups for three months… and then it finally ran out. God showed us that He was an 'above and beyond' God!

If you're ever in need of food, finances, or anything of the sort, just believe that God's got your back and that He is going to come through for you. If you need food, just pray over your cupboards and refrigerator, asking God to multiply the food that is there, and you will not run out. Do the same for your bank accounts. If you are a faithful Biblical Sower and you give 10% of your income to your church, or wherever else God tells you to give—because the church is not just a building; the church is actually people, in or out of church—then just know that God will bless your giving. And then you can claim that 'God meets all of my needs according to His riches and glory, by Christ Jesus' (see Philippians 4:19).

Just expect Him to do awesome things and He will! I give God all the praise and glory for it!

Personal Testimonials

David Hogan

A Missionary Evangelist in Mexico, David Hogan, is used by God for performing mighty amazing miracles! In his ministry, they have seen every single body part healed or recreated, over 700 people raised from the dead—some raised after being dead in the jungle for four days (which is very nasty).

I have watched approximately 450 of David's recorded sermons on YouTube videos, each approximately three hours long. After watching his videos, I use what I have learned from what he does in his healing ministry, and then I go out and literally practice the same methods on people here.

To be a missionary for David Hogan, you have to be able to raise the dead, heal the sick, cleanse a leper, and bring people to Christ; otherwise you don't qualify to be one of his missionaries.

The reason I mention David Hogan is that you can find him on YouTube and he will be a blessing to you, or you'll be offended, one or the other.

What God has done through that man is incredible. It's just totally incredible. And since I have been so blessed, and his ministry has helped my ministry as well, I just wanted to share this with you.

About John Beech – Life Story (as of September 17, 2022)

It started when I was five years old. My mom took me to the dentist and they put mercury fillings into my teeth…and it turned out that I was allergic to the mercury.

Now, years later, the doctor and I have traced back a lot of my medical problems since that day. And back then they didn't realize that mercury was bad for people. When it crosses the brain barrier, and I had a whole mouth full of it, it messes with your brain. Since I was five years old, I had all kinds of learning and reading problems all through school, and any sickness that came along I would get it because my immune system was compromised. At that time, the doctors didn't know what to do about it, and we didn't know anything about healing then.

My whole life, from age five, I had nothing but problems with sickness, going to the hospital, having all kinds of illnesses, had appendix removed, and kidney issues. Well, let's put it this way, there were well over a hundred problems that were wrong with me through the course of my life. It took a toll on going to school, people thought I was lying, teachers thought I was lying, and employers thought I was lying, because I was sick all the time. I had the best insurance that money could buy when I graduated from school, but it just wasn't enough to cover all the medical expenses. It took 66% of my income from three jobs to pay my portion of the medical bills when I was in my 20s.

I was having some problems with bleeding internally, so my doctor sent me to Mayo Clinic. They were able to locate where source of the bleeding and were able to fix it, but it took eight years to find that problem. And then I found out at the Mayo Clinic that I was born with a genetic problem which caused low testosterone and sterility. So, I found out at 19 years old that I would never have children. That was pretty devastating to hear that at 19 years old, but I kind of blew it off because I was 'young and dumb.' But as I started dating, I really loved this girl and wanted to marry her, but it was a problem with her mother because my girlfriend had wanted to have children her whole life but had never told me that. Then when our relationship got serious and I asked her father if I could marry her, he said yes. But then her mother came to see me, told me about my girlfriend's desire to have children, and it totally destroyed me.

One weekend when I was at her house, she and her mom came to me and told me about her wanting kids her whole life. I should have cut the relationship off right there and then, but I didn't... we loved each other. Knowing what I do now, I would never recommend to anyone to date for five years. My personal opinion is that if they can't make up their mind after a year or so, forget it.

I loved her, but she started dating someone else right after we broke up, and she ended up marrying him. She is happily married and has her children, and I'm happy for her. I hold nothing against her or her family at all.

But it wounded me deeply. I had 14 rounds of Pericarditis , which causes you to think you're having a heart attack but it's actually the lining of your heart that swells up and your heart rubs on that and it can kill you. Doctor's couldn't figure out where that came from, but eventually they figured out it was a parasitic germ that comes from Africa. But I had never been to Africa, nor did I know anyone who had been to Africa. The medicine the doctors gave me didn't work, and actually caused more problems. So I was finally able to kill that germ off by using Homeopathic treatments.

I won't bore you with all of the problems and sicknesses I've had…it's frankly too much.

I owed a quarter of a million dollars for medical bills. Someone walked into the hospital and paid $100,000 of the bill, and the hospital, as part of their agreement with the donor, couldn't tell me who blessed me! I worked for years to pay off all the rest of it, and by the grace of God, He helped me pay it all off. But it was like paying three mortgages. I had been to court, I had three

Personal Testimonials

judgements against me because of medical bills, and life had not been easy. At one point I worked five jobs when I felt healthy enough to do it, and trying to bury the pain of being rejected because I couldn't father children I just became a workaholic. And I just buried everything and that was what was killing me.

I didn't want to lose my condo because I still owed money on it. But God was providing the money as I needed it. And I never gave up; I totally relied on God. The older I get the more I totally rely on Jesus, and I can't wait to spend time with Him, and I sing songs to Him. He just always comes through for me. If you want to fail in life, give up.

Even though I was saved, I found out later that I hadn't been taught how to have a relationship with Jesus. But the Holy Spirit teaches us all things, and when I learned how to pray in the Spirit, it was a total game changer. I became extremely bold when witnessing to people. I could talk to anybody...and I mean anybody! I used to be afraid of people—I'm not anymore, especially when I'm talking about Jesus.

I had no clue about healing, but I am still learning. I believe we won't know everything until we get to heaven, so until then I keep trying and learning.

Somebody told me one time, "You need to stop praying for all these other people, and find out what the heck is wrong with you! Why do you keep getting sick?" I said, "Well, I'm not going to stop praying for people, even if I am sick because I don't care, it doesn't matter. I have a heart to see people healed, and especially saved!"

I did start asking God more about my own healing, and I started learning that demons can cause a lot of health problems, but I just had no clue. Around 2020, just before Covid hit, I had a major heart attack, and then a year later had another one during Covid, resulting with getting five stents inserted into my heart. Approximately six months later, I started having severe palpitations. I began to struggle with fear and had major panic attacks. It seemed that every day something nasty would happen to me. I mean, literally every day the devil was doing everything he could to take me out. And God healed me of it.

I had been doing self-deliverances on myself through the Internet, and demons had been coming out, and I had been getting a lot of change from that. But I knew what the problem was, but I didn't know how to get rid of it—I had the spirit of infirmity, which I later discovered comes through the womb, basically sins of your parents and previous ancestors. We don't know what all they were into. But...it's not their fault... we just didn't know.

So, in July, 2022, at 61 years old, I was invited to an outdoor tent revival service at a church in Hastings, Michigan. Jennifer Martin was the guest evangelist speaker, and I am telling you...God showed up! When I went to the meeting, I had six of the palpitation attacks that morning. Doctors didn't know what was causing it. They inserted a 2-inch-long loop recorder implant into my chest three days before the Friday night meeting to determine what was going on. At the meeting, my chest was all black-and-blue, I was on oxygen, and was not doing well. I couldn't work and had major health problems, including heart failure. I told God, "There is so much wrong with me that I don't know how to stay alive." Then I just relied on Jesus.

At that tent revival, the Glory of God showed up! It was incredible seeing so many miracles in so many people. It was amazing to see demons coming out of many people, and many miraculous healings.

I hadn't even been able to drive myself to those meetings. But God put friends around me who picked me up and brought me each night. I couldn't stand for long and had to sit down because I was in bad shape. One of Jennifer's prayer warriors approached my seat and prayed for me, and I literally shook for about three hours from the presence of God. The shaking stopped when I got home around 1:00 am. The presence was so strong. From that point on, I've only had to have oxygen once! I brought it with me to the Saturday night meeting to be on the safe side, but I left it in the car.

That night I shared with some others about my miraculous healing that took place the night before. Someone told Jennifer about it, so at the beginning of her 'service' she called me to the front to give testimony of my healing experience. While I was testifying, I pounded on my chest where the implant incision was and there was no pain, whereas the day before I needed pain medication to help with the pain.

Like I've said before, I had many other health problems besides the heart issues. So during the Saturday and Sunday night meetings, I experienced many more healings and deliverances, including God healing my Plantar fasciitis in my heel—the pain went away while I was standing there. I have not been sick since those meetings.

The pain in my heel occasionally comes back, but I talk to it and command it to leave in the name of Jesus, and it leaves! I've had migraines trying to come on me, because I dealt with someone who had migraines, so I pray against them and they're gone! So, Satan still tries to attack, but now I use my God-given authority and it leaves quickly, in Jesus' name!

It's been several months since those meetings and healings, and I feel better and stronger every day! So much so, that I cleared the long lot line behind the senior condominium complex where I live. It required 40-60 dead trees to be cut down and hauled away, branch debris removed from building roofs, and gutters cleared out. A huge job!

One day while I was on a garage roof cutting limbs 10 feet above me, I had no problems at all. Don't get me wrong, I was tired and had to sit down every once in a while, but you know...for three weeks I worked on that project with a few younger guys that helped haul brush, and I just got stronger every day.

One of the guys helping was handicapped. He remarked that I talk to Jesus and that Holy Spirit all the time. I answered, "Yes! Because He's protecting me up here."

After that tree clearing project was complete, I felt so strong that I knew I was ready to go back to work. I asked God for a specific type of job, not a large warehouse, not too many people around, and something I could do. God blessed me with a job and I'm thriving at it; so much so that the owner and people in the office are all talking about it.

I've always had kind of a problem working for others because I had so much trouble when I got sick so often. So I had gone into business for myself so if I needed a day off because I was sick, I could take a day off.

But you know...God is so good, and I testify of His goodness all the time. I am still learning, still seeking God, and He's doing incredible things in my life.

That Saturday night at the revival meeting, the church's pastor came to talk with me and a friend. This friend had been into a different type of religion and was freed from it as he was delivered of demons.

I mentioned to the pastor that I had been writing a book of personal testimonial stories which covered an 11-year period, which I had written during the Covid lockdown period. He showed me some of his own published books, and told me he would share the name of his editor who may be able to help me get my book published. So he e-mailed her information to me the next week.

I contacted the editor and arranged a meeting so I could bring my book's manuscript to her on a digital flash drive. While I was at her house I shared some testimonial stories that I hadn't, at that time, included in my book.

After the editor had done the editing process on the book, she printed the first draft for me and we met again. She suggested adding more stories before we published it, and asked how I felt about that idea. I wasn't sure about it at first. Her husband had a word for me that I should get a recorder to record more stories, and the editor was willing to transcribe and type them if I did.

Personal Testimonials

After I brought the draft home and read through it myself, I was really enthralled with the stories, but then when they ended, I understood what the editor meant about needing more stories.

Well, since technology isn't always my friend, and it had taken me a long time (not without struggling), to type the stories I had, I knew it would take me a long time to type more. I was also hesitant to agree to add more stories because I hadn't heard from the Lord that it was OK to add more. So I went before the Lord and asked Him, "Is it OK to use other testimonies other than those three years' stories?" He said, "Yes."

Since I work only three days a week, I have a pretty tight budget and I didn't have the money to buy a recorder, so I asked the Lord for the money to buy one. Amazingly, God provided the money the next day, a Saturday, within two hours! And by 1:00 that afternoon, I had ordered a recorder.

In order to record more testimonies, I have to pray in the Spirit and ask the Holy Spirit to remind me of the details and what was said, because when I minister to people, later I don't always remember everything I've said because He was flowing through me at those times. He does bring it all back to my remembrance as I speak about them into the recorder.

As my editor transcribed these stories from my recordings, she had to siphon through all my stories to help me get them on paper so they sound and look good. And that is the reason you're reading this book now.

I give all the praise and honor to the glory of God for what he's done in my life. It feels so good to not have to go to the doctor, and not have to pay hundreds of thousands of dollars for medical care. People have been 'coming out of the woodwork' and have given me money to live on above and beyond my 3-day-a-week job. And the reason that is happening is that I told God what I financially needed. I commanded the devil to get his hands out of my wallet and out of my investments, and out of my life. I commanded the Angels to go get all the financial losses from not being able to work...all of that...and bring the money to me. And God's starting to do that.

It's incredible! How touching that is see God moving financially for me.

The Lord is not done with me yet. I feel stronger, and my muscles feel stronger, every day. I'm healthy, and it's great to not need an oxygen tank any more. God's been healing a lot of areas in my life even now; the diseases and other medical issues that are still present.

God led me to a heart doctor from the United Kingdom who told me that if I cut out caffeine, use a magnesium spray across the top of my diaphragm before going to bed, go to bed an hour earlier than usual, and exercise a little, that the palpitations would stop. Well, I did

Personal Testimonials

what he advised and they did stop! And then I've experimented a little. I enjoy a good cup of coffee and diet Coke, so I drank some late in the day, and sure enough...I had palpitations. But if I drink anything with caffeine early in the morning it doesn't bother me. I thank God for showing me that.

I still pray for others. God delivered four more people, just this week, of demons. I just give God all the praises, honor and glory for it.

I continue to ask God to allow me, during my lifetime, to see every single body part that I pray for healed or re-created, and I want to raise people (and animals) from the dead. Especially, I want to see hundreds and thousands of people saved.

I would like to give away millions and millions of dollars for the Kingdom, through inventions and business, and the wealth transfer that is coming soon. I want to be able to buy houses for people. I've helped widows my whole life, but I want to help more. I want to help divorced and single moms more because most have a rough life and they deserve better. I've asked God to use me in those ways to bring souls into the Kingdom through business or whatever He wants me to do, I'm willing.

This is the end of this testimony as of September 19th, 2022, but life is going on. I believe that we're going to be able to go to the nations. I don't know what that will look like, but I've asked God for the nations. I want to see people saved, healed, delivered, set free; the torments gone out of their minds. I want to see people out of wheelchairs, amputees' limbs grow out, and for military trauma that was experienced which caused PTSD gone, and their lives healed, restored, and especially having a relationship with Jesus! That's the most important.

I thank you for reading my book, and I pray you would make a decision for Jesus. Jesus Christ is the only way to heaven; there is no other way, call on His name, ask Him to reveal Himself to you, and He will. And then get the Baptism of the Holy Spirit—explained those things in the back of this book

Thank you, I hope you enjoyed my book.

Blessings to you all in Jesus' Name.

~John Beech

In closing...

There are many more miraculous experiences that the Lord allowed me to witness and be a part of. I am humbled, honored, and blessed that He chose me to help His people. He never ceases to amaze me with His love, compassion, and great works of healing.

I pray that these stories have been a blessing for you, and an inspiration to increase your trust and faith in God.

As you continue with Parts 2 and 3, and as God speaks to you, I pray that you will allow Him to move upon your heart to accomplish His will for your life.

Part 2

Plan of Salvation

Receive Jesus as Your Personal Savior

Choosing to receive Jesus Christ as your Lord and Savior is the most important decision you will ever make. God's word promises that:

> [9]*"If you confess with your mouth the Lord Jesus and believe in your heart that God has raised Him from the dead, you will be saved.* [10]*For with the heart one believes unto righteousness and with the mouth confession is made unto salvation."*
>
> — *Romans 10:9-10*

> *"For whoever calls on the name of the Lord shall be saved."*
>
> — *Romans 10:13*

By His grace, God has already done everything to provide salvation; your part is simply to believe and receive.

Pray this simple prayer out loud:

"Jesus, I confess that You are my Lord and

Plan of Salvation

Savior. I believe in my heart that Jesus raised You from the dead. By faith in Your word, I receive salvation now. Thank You for saving me, King Jesus."

Now that you are saved, if you don't already have a Bible, you need to get one. I suggest the New King James version or the Amplified Bible.

Start by reading the Gospel of John 1:1. After that, ask the Holy Spirit to show you where and what to read next.

Part 3

Receive the Holy Spirit

Praying in the Spirit

As His child, your loving heavenly Father wants to give you the supernatural power you need to live this new life.

> *"For everyone who asks receives, and he who seeks finds, and to him who knocks it will be opened."*
>
> — *Matthew 7:8*

All you have to do is ask, believe and receive.

Pray this prayer: Father, I recognize my need for Your power to live this new life. Please fill me with Your Holy Spirit. By faith, I receive it right now. Thank You for baptizing me, Holy Spirit. You are welcome into my life.

Congratulations, now you are filled with God's supernatural power. Some syllables from a language you don't recognize will rise from your heart into your mouth.

> *"For if I pray in a tongue, my spirit prays, but my understanding is unfruitful."*
>
> — *I Corinthians 14:14*

As you speak them out loud by faith, you're releasing God's power from within and building yourself up in your spirit.

> *"He who speaks in a tongue edifies himself, but he who prophesies edifies the Church."*
>
> — I Corinthians 14:4

It doesn't matter whether you felt anything or not when you prayed to receive the Lord and his Spirit. If you believed in your heart that you received, then God's word promises that you did.

> *"Therefore I say to you whatever things you ask when you pray, believe that you receive them and you will have them."*
>
> — Mark 11:24

You can pray in the Spirit whenever and wherever you like.

God always honors His word—believe it.

Made in the USA
Monee, IL
12 January 2023